DRIP DROP

WATER'S JOURNEY

EVE & ALBERT STWERTKA
PICTURES BY MENA DOLOBOWSKY

JULIAN Ⓜ MESSNER

Text copyright © 1991 by Eve and
Albert Stwertka
Illustrations copyright © 1991 by
Mena Dolobowsky
All rights reserved including the
right of reproduction in whole or in
part in any form. Published by Julian
Messner, a division of Silver Burdett
Press, Inc., Simon & Schuster, Inc.
Prentice Hall Bldg., Englewood
Cliffs, NJ 07632.

JULIAN MESSNER and colophon are
trademarks of Simon & Schuster, Inc.

Design by Malle N. Whitaker.
Manufactured in the United States
of America.

Lib. ed.
10 9 8 7 6 5 4 3 2 1
Paper ed.
10 9 8 7 6 5 4 3 2 1

**Library of Congress
Cataloging-in-Publication Data**
Stwertka, Eve.
    Drip drop : water's journey /
Eve and Albert Stwertka.
        p.   cm. — (At home with
science)
    Includes index.
    Summary: Explains the basic
properties of water, as well as
how it is treated and piped to
and from the home.
    1. Municipal water supply—
Juvenile literature.   2. Water—
Juvenile literature.   [1. Water
supply.   2. Water.]   I. Stwertka,
Albert.   II. Title.   III. Series.
TD348.S78 1991   90-39301
628.1—dc20   CIP AC
ISBN 0-671-69456-1 (lib. ed.)
ISBN 0-671-69462-6 (paper ed.)

CONTENTS

WATER TAKES A TRIP

Three cheers for a splash in the bathtub after a day of work and play! Open the tap just a little, and big drops of water come out. Open the tap wider. The drops turn into a trickle, a stream, a gushing waterfall.

Water flows to your home, serves your needs, then disappears. Where does it come from? Where does it go? Let's start with the first question.

To reach your house, water takes a long journey. It starts from rivers and lakes, or from wells deep in the earth.

At the treatment center, workers test the water and make it safe for drinking. From there, it rushes through tunnels, under fields and streets, and up into metal pipes inside your walls. It rests in the pipes until you let it run into your sink, tub, toilet, or washing machine.

Is this the end of the water journey? No. The trip goes on.

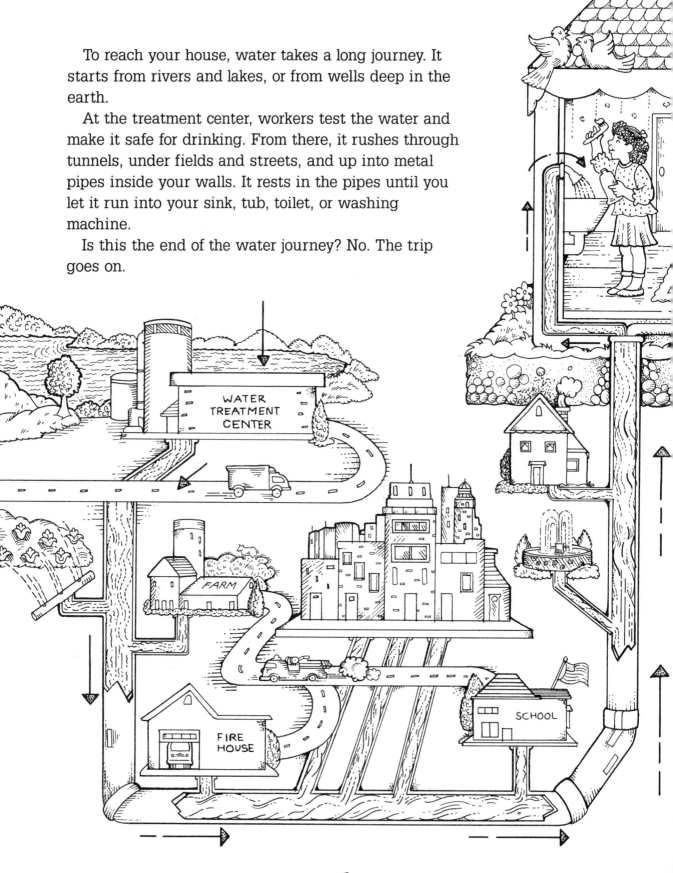

Clean water reaches your house through one set of pipes. The used water runs out through a different set.

The soapy water from your bath gurgles down the drain. It travels through underground sewer pipes. The next stop is the pollution control center. Here, the water is cleaned and set free again to splash outdoors.

But the water journey is still not over.

What can you do with water?

Wash my bike.
Paint pictures.
What else?
Add to this list.

Squirt!!

I can water my flowers!

POLLUTION CONTROL CENTER

Evaporation and Condensation

Did you know that more than three-fourths of the earth's surface is ocean? When the sun heats the ocean, the water changes. It turns into a gas called **water vapor** that rises into the air. The change of water from a liquid to a gas is called **evaporation.**

You cannot see water vapor. Sometimes, though, the vapor meets air that is cooler. Then the vapor changes again. It turns into drops of water that hang in the air like tiny balloons. The change of water vapor into drops of water is called **condensation.**

When the drops hang near the ground, we call them mist, fog, or steam. When they form high above the earth, they become the clouds you see in the sky.

If the clouds meet even colder air, they condense some more. The drops bond together into bigger drops that are too heavy to hang in the sky. Down they fall. It is raining.

Sometimes the drops freeze and come down as hail or sleet. Sometimes they form beautiful flakes of snow.

But soon, the water on roofs and streets evaporates and forms new clouds. Ice and snow melt. The fresh water fills rivers, pours into lakes and oceans, or sinks into the earth.

Is the water journey finally over? You might have guessed that the answer is no. Water evaporates and condenses over and over again. It is on a round trip without end. We call it **the water cycle.**

The Forms of Water

Water takes many forms. It can be a liquid, a solid, or a gas.

Try this...

Fill a plastic or paper cup two-thirds full of water. Put the cup in your freezer. An hour later, you'll have a cup of ice. Keep the ice at room temperature. Soon it will be a liquid again.

Pour a little of the water into a saucer and let it stand. The next day, the saucer will be empty. The water has turned into a gas and escaped into the air.

It escaped!!

THE NEXT DAY

11

Copy the weather!

Pour three cups of water into a pot. Ask an adult to help you boil the water on the stove. Soon, steam will rise from the pot. (Steam is hot, so watch out for your arms and face.) Now you have fog and clouds in your kitchen.

Remove the pot from the stove. Put a cover on it for two minutes. Because the pot cover is cooler than the steam, the water vapor condenses and forms drops. Lift the cover and shake it over the sink to let the drops fall.

Now you are making rain.

12

Water and Life

Milk, juice, or soda—whatever you drink is made up mainly of water. Even the foods you eat contain water. If you didn't have water for a day or two, you would get very thirsty, then very sick.

In fact, two-thirds of your body is made up of water. All animals and plants need water to live, even the smallest germs.

No wonder I'm hungry! My lunch was mostly water!

Plants draw water from the soil through their roots and stems. At the same time, they give up water through their leaves to the air around them.

Try this...

Cut the tops off two carrots. Leave a little of the green stems. Put each carrot top in a small dish. Add a little water to one dish, but leave the other dish dry. Now place both dishes in a sunny place.

A carrot is a root that draws up water to nourish its green plant. In five or six days, new leaves will start to sprout from the plant that has water. The dry plant, though, will be all shriveled up.

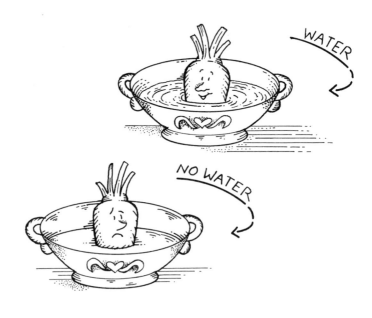

WATER

NO WATER

FIVE DAYS LATER...

I'm dying of THIRST!

You, too, take in water by eating and drinking. Then you return it to the water cycle when you breathe, sweat, and urinate.

Try this...

Breathe gently on a mirror. You can see some of the water in your body come out and condense on the cool glass.

In cold weather, notice how the water drops in your breath form mist in the air.

15

WATER COMES TO YOUR HOUSE

Where many people live together, they need a large supply of clean water. Some cities bring in water from nearby rivers. Others fence in lakes to make **reservoirs** that store water. Sometimes, people dig wells to look for water inside the earth.

Where does your water come from?

A reservoir?
Or a well?
Or a river?
Or....?
Check with your water company to find out.

In many places, the ground holds moisture close to the surface. If we drill fifty to a hundred feet into the earth, the **groundwater** seeps in and collects to form a well.

In other places, water is hidden more than a thousand feet down. It lies in spongy layers of soil, between other layers of rock or clay. These deep water layers are called **aquifers.**

The Top level of ground water is called the **water table**

Well

Well

Earth and Sand

Sand

Ground water

Clay

Clay

Rock

Aquifer

Rock

At the Water Treatment Center

Most water needs treatment before it is fit to drink. At the treatment center, workers test the water to see if any germs or plants live in it.

They also make sure no harmful chemicals from factories have seeped in. Near the ocean, they test for traces of salt.

The workers may treat the water with a chemical called **alum.** It makes the dirt stick together in soft clumps that sink to the bottom of the water tank.

Next, the water sinks through layers of fine, clean sand. The sand filters out small impurities.

Try this...

Mix one tablespoon of potting soil with a cup of water. Fasten a paper towel over the mouth of a jar. Use a rubber band. Push the towel in a little at the center. Now pour the water mixture slowly into the jar.

The muddy soil stays in the towel filter. The water in the jar is almost clear again.

Sometimes, air is sent bubbling through the water.
This improves the color and taste.

20

To make sure no germs can live in the water, workers add a chemical called **chlorine.** Many cities also add **fluoride,** which can prevent tooth cavities.

The last test is for acids that might damage water pipes and cause other problems. If the acid level is too high, another chemical must be added to lower it.

Now the water is safe for bathing and drinking. It can flow to your house.

21

Pumps and Pressure

Why does water run out of the tap as soon as you open it? It is under pressure. One way to put water under pressure is to push it with a pump.

A pump places force on the water, which makes it spurt out of the nearest opening.

Strong electric pumps can draw up water from deep underground. They can make it run uphill or to the top of a skyscraper.

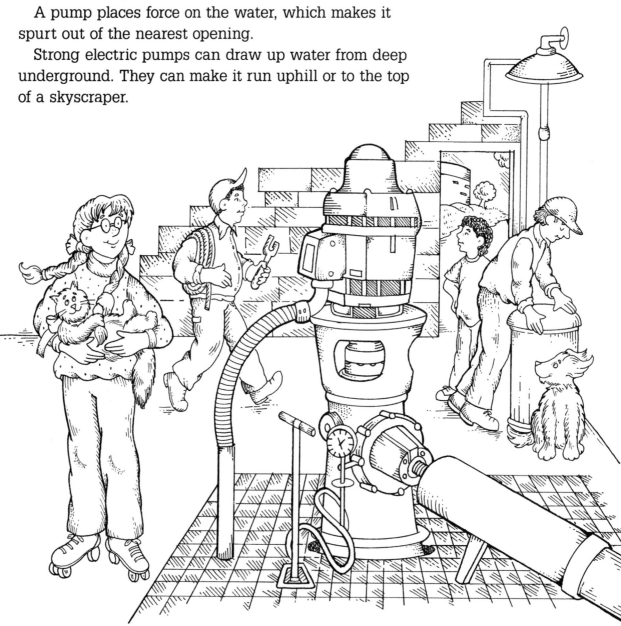

22

FLEXIBLE
STRAW

TAPE

Try this...

You can make a simple pump with an empty milk carton.

Fill the carton about half full of water.

Place the carton on its back. Hold it over the sink, with the open spout facing up.

Tape it shut with water-proof tape, but leave a small gap at the top.

Slip a flexible straw through the gap. Bend it to make a spout. Then tape it in place.

PUSH DOWN HERE

Push down hard on the carton a few times. Why does the water spurt out? The air you are squeezing together puts pressure on the water and forces it through the opening.

Gravity

There is another way to build up **water pressure.** Use the natural force of **gravity.** Things fall when you don't hold them up because they are pulled down by this powerful force.

Water, too, is pulled by gravity. As water falls, it gathers energy that enables it to rise again.

We use this energy when we bring down water from a reservoir high in the mountains to a city in the valley below. The water rushes downhill and builds up enough pressure to rise several floors in the pipes of the houses.

Try this...

Buy a piece of half-inch plastic tube at the hardware store. You'll need about 2½ feet.

Cut the top off a milk carton. Make a small hole near the bottom.

Fit one end of the tube in the hole and tape it water-tight. This is your reservoir.

Tie the other end of the tube to the sink faucet. The middle part of the tube should hang down in the sink.

Now raise the carton high above the faucet while you pour in water from a glass. You'll see the water spurt up under pressure.

Lower your "reservoir" and you are lowering the pressure. When you bring the carton down to the level of the faucet, the water stops running.

25

Tall buildings often keep a supply of water in a storage tank on the roof. Look for these roof tanks high above city streets.

Many towns keep huge storage towers filled with water for emergencies.

Pipes and Valves

The pipes that bring water to a big city may be wide enough for you to stand in. In fact, New York City's water tunnels are so large that a truck could drive through them!

Narrower pipes carry the water to the different streets. From here, even thinner pipes run into the houses.

All these pipes are full of water under pressure.

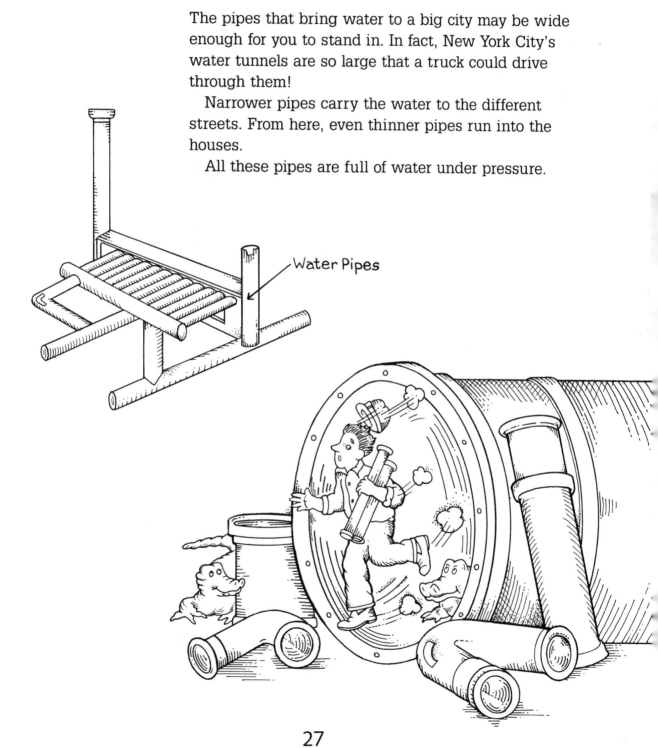

Water Pipes

With so much pressure in the pipes, what stops the water from pouring out in a flood? The device that holds it back is called a **valve.**

A valve is a strong, tight gate set between sections of the pipe. Open the gate and the water runs out. Close it and the water stops.

Your hand on the sink faucet controls a valve. Washing machines, dishwashers, toilets, and fire hydrants are all turned on and off by valves.

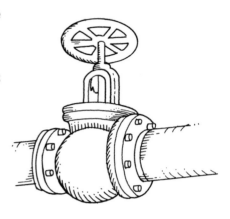

WHEEL

STEM

CLOSED

OPEN

QUICK!
I Need
A VALVE!

WATER TAKES A BATH

After washing laundry and dishes, flushing toilets, and cleaning floors, the water is full of soap and dirt. It may also be polluted with paint, grease, and chemicals.

Polluted water kills fish. It also makes people sick after they swim or eat fresh- or salt-water fish. Before we can send used water back to nature, it needs cleaning.

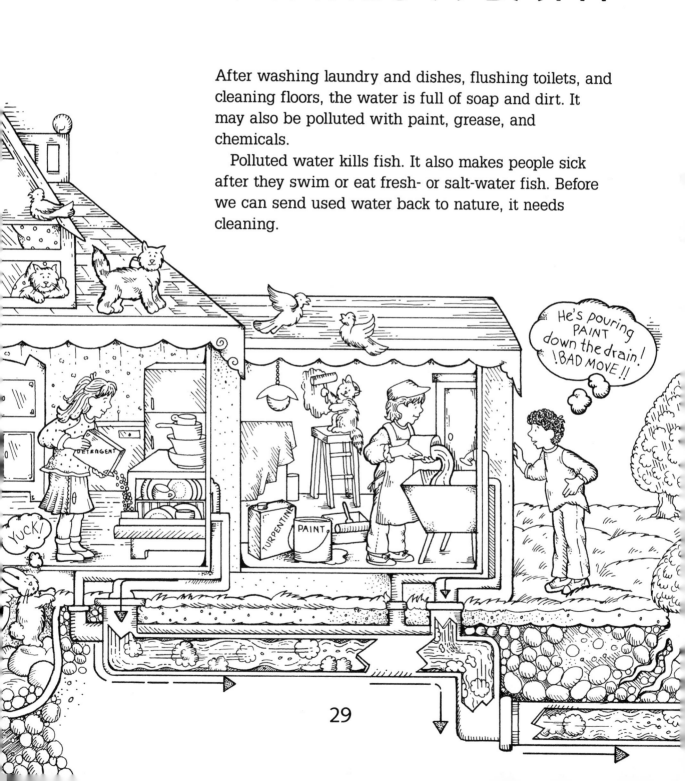

29

At The Pollution Control Center

Do you live in the country? If so, the waste water from your house probably runs to a **septic tank** buried in your backyard. In towns or cities, though, the waste water runs down to large sewer pipes under the streets.

The sewers pick up sewage or liquid wastes from homes, restaurants, hospitals, and factories. The waste water is then carried to a central place for cleaning.

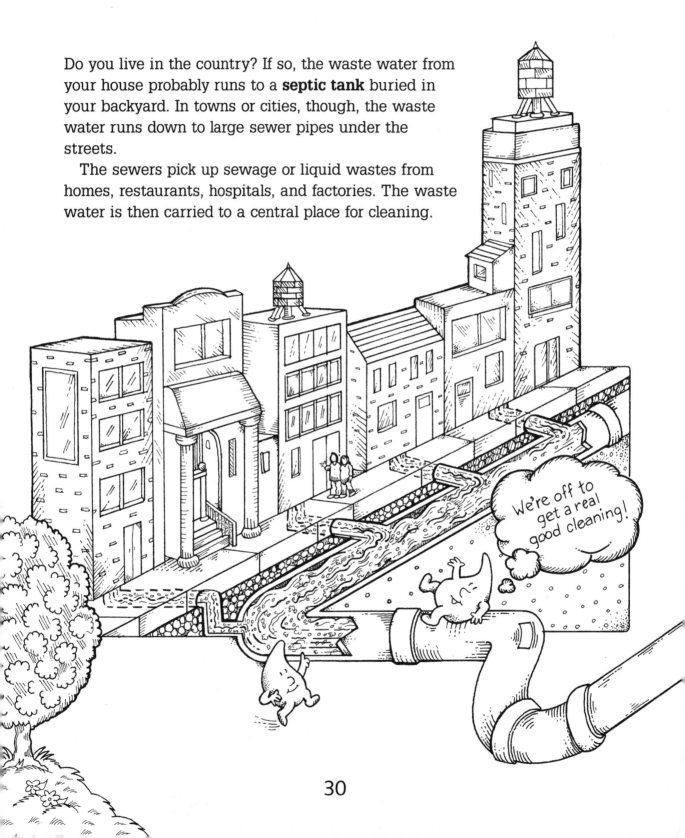

We're off to get a real good cleaning!

When the dirty water reaches the pollution control center, it first runs through a screen and past a cutter that chops up the pieces of paper. Then the water flows to a **settling tank** that looks like a huge concrete swimming pool. Here it rests, so that the heavy **sludge** can sink to the bottom.

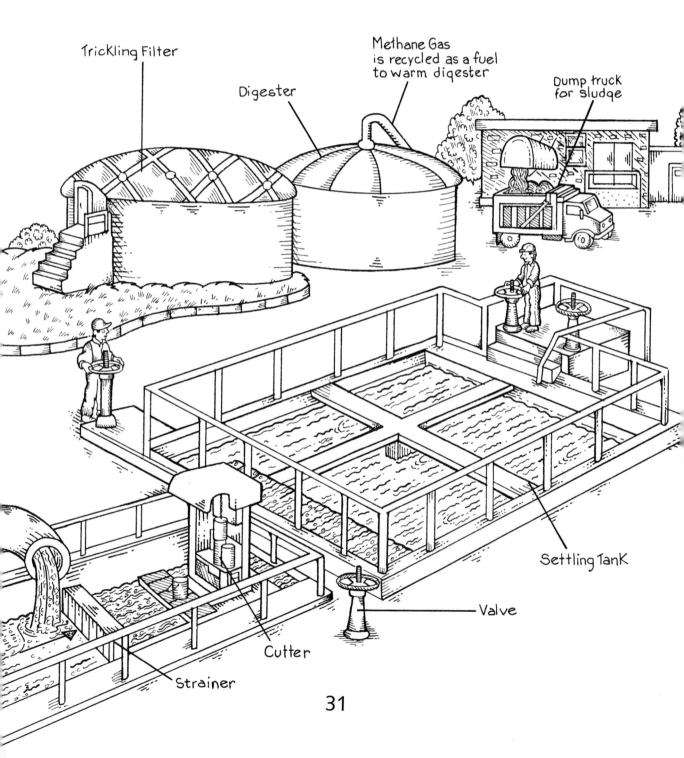

Trickling Filter

Digester

Methane Gas is recycled as a fuel to warm digester

Dump truck for sludge

Settling Tank

Valve

Cutter

Strainer

Try this...

To see how a settling tank works, mix a tablespoon of potting soil with a cup of water. Shake it up in a jar, then let it stand. Notice how quickly the water clears. Time it.

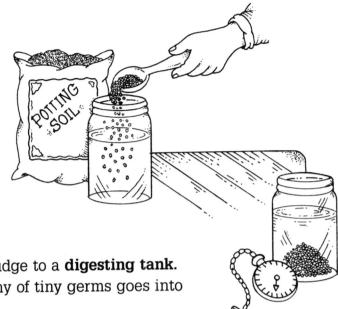

Next, workers pump the sludge to a **digesting tank.** Inside the closed tank, an army of tiny germs goes into action.

Germs feed on all kinds of waste matter. By digesting the sludge, they make it less harmful. At the same time, they create a smelly gas called **methane** that is quite useful. Methane can be burned as a fuel.

Later, the sludge dries out. Workers drive it away and dump it at a landfill.

Meanwhile, the partly cleared water runs underground. It travels to a round stone building full of rocks. This is the **trickling filter.**

Pumps force the water to rise through a pipe in the center. At the top, it sprays out over the rocks and trickles to the bottom.

Billions of germs live among these slimy rocks. They devour bits of waste in the water and do an important cleanup job.

Next, there's a second turn in a settling tank. Then the water passes through a filter of fine sand. Finally, it takes a long bath in a tank filled with chlorine. Any germs that might have escaped the sand filter are killed.

A worker checks the tester to see if everything is in order.

At last, a worker opens a valve. The clean water splashes outdoors again, into the river, lake, or ocean. But the water journey is not over. As you know, the next stage is about to begin.

Saving Every Drop

The amount of water in the world never changes. However, the number of people who need it keeps growing.

Besides, most of the world's water is not available for drinking. Ninety-seven percent lies in the salty oceans. Some of the rest is in clouds, icebergs, and glaciers.

Now add pollution to the problem. You will see why good water is so precious.

Be a Pollution Fighter!

Don't Pour These Down the Drain:

House paints
Cleaning fluid
Gasoline
Grease

Don't Waste Water!

Keep your shower short.

Take a mini-bath.

Don't run the water while you brush your teeth.

Report leaking pipes and taps.

If you don't finish a glass of water, give the rest to a plant.

Collect rainwater to pour on your garden.

What other water saving tips can you think of?

WATER WORDS

Alum (AL-um)—a chemical added to water at a treatment center. Alum makes coarse dirt stick together in clumps for easy removal.

Aquifer (AK-wa-fer)—a layer of water found deep under the ground among rocks or soil.

Chlorine (KLOR-een)—a chemical added to water at a treatment center. Most cities have chlorine in their drinking water.

Condensation (kon-den-SAY-shun)—the change in form water goes through when it turns from a gas to a liquid.

Digesting Tank—a closed tank where sewage is digested by germs, broken down, and made less harmful.

Evaporation (ee-vap-uh-RAY-shun)—the change in form water goes through when it turns from a liquid to a gas.

Fluoride (FLOR-ide)—a chemical many cities add to drinking water to help people avoid getting cavities.

Gravity (GRAV-uh-tee)—the force in nature that pulls things towards the earth and makes them "fall."

Groundwater—water the soil holds like a sponge just below the surface of the ground.

Methane (METH-ane)—the natural gas formed when sewage is broken down by germs. It can be burned as a fuel.

Reservoir (REZ-a-vwar)—a natural or artificial lake that collects and stores water for use by a city.

Septic tank—a tank, usually underground, where wastewater from a house is broken down and purified by germs.

Settling tank—a large, concrete pool for sewage. Heavy sludge settles to the bottom of the pool.

Sewage (SOO-ij)—the liquid wastes that run out through the sewers of a town or city.

Sludge (sluj)—the heavy waste that settles to the bottom of a settling tank in a water treatment center.

Trickling Filter—a round building where water is treated by trickling slowly among rocks. Germs, which cover the rocks, digest the wastes in the water.

Valve—a device to control the amount of water flowing through a pipe.

Water cycle—the movement of water in its different forms (liquid, gas, or frozen solid) from the earth to the sky and back again.

Water pressure—the force that water places on any surface it comes in contact with.

Water vapor—water in the form of a gas.

39

INDEX